For exams in 2022

ICAEW
Assurance

First edition 2007, Fifteenth edition 2021

ISBN 9781 5097 3842 7

British Library Cataloguing-in-Publication Data

A catalogue record for this book is available from the British Library

Published by

BPP Learning Media Ltd
BPP House, Aldine Place
142–144 Uxbridge Road
London W12 8AA

www.bpp.com/learningmedia

Printed in the United Kingdom

Your learning materials, published by BPP Learning Media Ltd, are printed on paper obtained from traceable sustainable sources.

The content of this publication is intended to prepare students for the ICAEW examinations, and should not be used as professional advice. Although every effort has been made to ensure that the contents of this book are correct at the time of going to press, BPP Learning Media makes no warranty that the information in this book is accurate or complete and accepts no liability for any loss or damage suffered by any person acting or refraining from acting as a result of the material in this book.

ICAEW takes no responsibility for the content of any supplemental training materials supplied by the Partner in Learning.

The ICAEW Partner in Learning logo, ACA and ICAEW CFAB are all registered trademarks of ICAEW and are used under licence by BPP Learning Media Ltd.

Welcome to BPP Learning Media's **Passcards** for ICAEW **Assurance**.

- They **save you time**. Important topics are summarised for you.

- They incorporate **diagrams** to kick start your memory.

- They follow the overall **structure** of the ICAEW Workbook, but BPP Learning Media's ICAEW **Passcards** are not just a condensed book. Each card has been separately designed for clear presentation. Topics are self-contained and can be grasped visually.

- ICAEW **Passcards** are **just the right size** for pockets, briefcases and bags.

- ICAEW **Passcards focus on the exams** you will be facing.

Run through the **Passcards** as often as you can during your final revision period. The day before the exam, try to go through the **Passcards** again! You will then be well on your way to passing your exams.

Good luck!

Preface

Contents

1: Concept of and need for assurance

Topic List

What is assurance?

Levels of assurance

Examples

Audit

Benefits and limitations

This chapter provides an introduction into why there is a need for assurance services, for example, audit and review. It is important that you have grasped the key auditing concepts outlined in this chapter because it is the foundation for the rest of your studies.

Assurance engagement: one in which a practitioner expresses a conclusion designed to enhance the degree of confidence of the intended users other than the responsible party about the outcome of the evaluation or measurement of a subject matter against criteria.

Elements of an assurance engagement

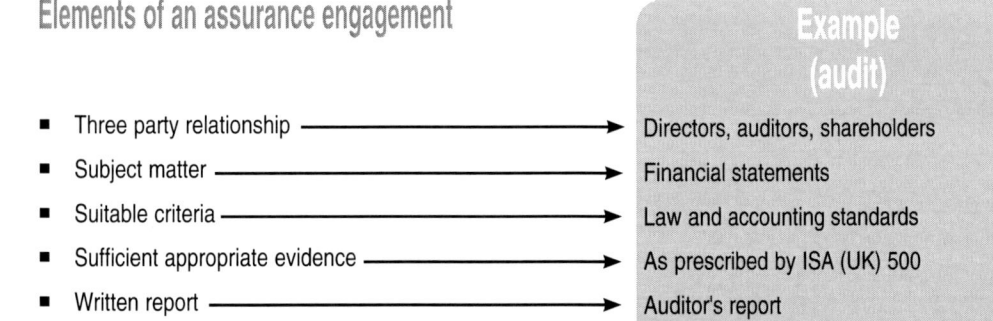

Example (audit)

- Three party relationship ⟶ Directors, auditors, shareholders
- Subject matter ⟶ Financial statements
- Suitable criteria ⟶ Law and accounting standards
- Sufficient appropriate evidence ⟶ As prescribed by ISA (UK) 500
- Written report ⟶ Auditor's report

Type of engagement	Evidence sought	Conclusion given	Example
Reasonable assurance	Sufficient and appropriate	Positive form of words	In my opinion, the statement by the Chairman regarding X is reasonable
Limited assurance	Sufficient and appropriate (lower level)	Negative form of words	In the course of my seeking evidence about the statement by the Chairman, nothing has come to my attention indicating that the statement is not reasonable

| What is assurance? | Levels of assurance | **Examples** | Audit | Benefits and limitations |

Audit

- Statutory audit
- Local authority audit
- Insurance company audit
- Bank audit
- Pension scheme audit
- Charity audit
- Solicitors' audit
- Environmental audit
- Branch audit

Assurance

- Value for money studies
- Circulation reports
- Cost/benefit reports
- Due diligence
- Internal audit
- Fraud investigations
- Internal control reports
- Reports on business plans/projections
- Website security reports

Audit of financial statements: an exercise whose objective is to enable the auditor to express an opinion whether the financial statements are prepared, in all material respects, in accordance with an applicable financial reporting framework.

True: information is factual and conforms with reality, not false. In addition it conforms with required standards and law. The accounts have been correctly extracted from the books and records.

Fair: information is free from discrimination and bias and complies with expected standards/rules. The accounts should reflect the commercial substance of the company's underlying transactions

The phrases used to express the auditor's opinion are **'give a true and fair view'** or **'present fairly, in all material respects'**, which are equivalent terms.

Auditors do not bear any responsibility for the preparation and presentation of the financial statements, which is the **responsibility of the directors**.

1: Concept of and need for assurance

Expectations gap: the gap between what the assurance provider understands he is doing and what the user of the information believes the assurance provider is doing.

Benefits

- Independent, professional verification
- Added confidence to other users
- Enhances credibility of information
- Helps prevent error/fraud
- Draws user's attention to deficiencies where they exist

Limitations

- Not all items in FS checked
- Limitations of systems
- Most evidence is persuasive rather than conclusive
- Chance of collusion in fraud
- Reliance on responsible party for correct information
- Estimates
- Subjective
- Limitations of assurance report

2: Process of assurance: obtaining an engagement

This chapter contains details of how to screen and accept a new client.

| Client screening | Client acceptance | Audit engagement letter |

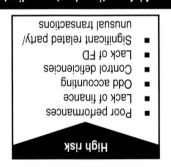

Factors for consideration
- Management integrity
- Risk
- Relationships
- Ability to perform the work
- Engagement economics

High risk
- Poor performances
- Lack of finance
- Odd accounting
- Control deficiencies
- Lack of FD
- Significant related party/ unusual transactions

Low risk
- Good prospects
- Well-financed
- Strong internal controls
- Prudent accounting
- Competent directors
- No unusual transactions

Sources of information about new clients

Enquiries of other sources (bankers, solicitors)

Review of **documents** (most recent annual accounts, listing particulars, credit rating)

Previous auditors (previous auditors should be invited to disclose fully all relevant information)

Review of **rules/standards** (consider specific laws/standards that relate to industry)

Before acceptance

The auditors should:

- Ensure **professionally qualified** to act ───
- Ensure **existing resources adequate** ───
- **Obtain references** ───
- **Communicate with present auditors** ───

■ Consider whether disqualified on legal or ethical grounds

■ Consider available time, staff and technical expertise

■ Make independent enquiries if directors not personally known

■ Enquire whether there are reasons/circumstances behind the change which the new auditors ought to know

After acceptance

The auditors should:

- Ensure outgoing auditors' removal/resignation properly conducted
- Ensure the new auditors' appointment is valid
- Set up and submit a letter of engagement

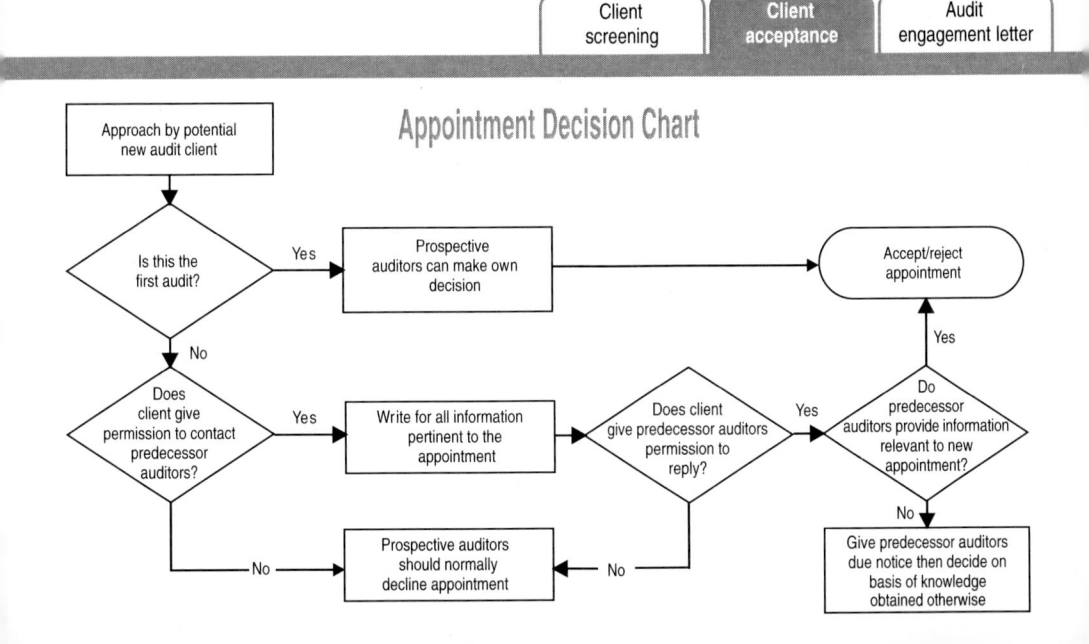

Appointment Decision Chart

Approach by potential new audit client

Is this the first audit? — **Yes** → Prospective auditors can make own decision → Accept/reject appointment

No

Does client give permission to contact predecessor auditors? — **Yes** → Write for all information pertinent to the appointment → Does client give predecessor auditors permission to reply? — **Yes** → Do predecessor auditors provide information relevant to new appointment? — **Yes** → Accept/reject appointment

No → Prospective auditors should normally decline appointment ← **No**

Do predecessor auditors provide information relevant to new appointment? — **No** → Give predecessor auditors due notice then decide on basis of knowledge obtained otherwise

Audit engagement letter: ISA (UK) 210 requires the auditor to agree the terms of the audit engagement with management in writing. This agreement is normally in the form of an audit engagement letter.

Contents of audit engagement letter

- Objective of the audit
- Scope of the audit
- Auditor's responsibility
- Applicable reporting framework, eg, IFRS
- Management's responsibility
- Form of any reports resulting from the engagement

Notes

3: Process of assurance: planning the assignment

Topic List

Planning

Analytical procedures

Materiality

Risk

Fraud

Every piece of assurance work carried out by a firm should be planned. Planning and risk are key areas for assurance providers.

| Planning | Analytical procedures | Materiality | Risk | Fraud |

Audit strategy – key elements

- **Understanding the entity and its environment**
  Industry conditions, client characteristics, management competence, accounting systems and policies.

- **Risk and materiality**
  Risks of fraud and error, significant and complex audit areas, setting materiality levels.

- **Practical matters**
  Timings, locations, staffing, reporting.

Auditors should plan the audit so that the engagement will be performed in an effective manner (ISA (UK) 300).

Aim: to **reduce audit risk** to an acceptably low level.

Objectives of planning

- Ensuring attention devoted to specific areas of risk
- Potential problems identified
- Ensuring audit properly organised and managed
- Work is assigned to team members properly
- Facilitating review of work

Audit plan: sets out the nature, timing and extent of audit procedures to be performed by engagement team members in order to obtain sufficient appropriate audit evidence.

ISA (UK) 315.11

The objective of the auditor is to identify and assess the risks of material misstatement, whether due to fraud or error, at the financial statement and assertion levels thereby providing a basis for designing and implementing responses to the assessed risks of material misstatement.

Procedures to carry out:

- Enquires of management/others in entity
- Analytical procedures
- Observation and inspection

They may also perform other procedures where circumstances merit it.

The auditor performs **risk assessment procedures** that allow them to identify and assess the risks of material misstatement, and design further audit procedures (ISA (UK) 315: para. 13). Procedures must **not** be biased towards obtaining evidence that is **corroborative**, and which excludes contradictory evidence.

The engagement team should discuss how the financial reporting framework applies, and the susceptibility to material misstatement (ISA (UK) 315: para. 17).

Matters of which to gain understanding (from ISA (UK) 315)

The entity and its environment, and the FR framework

- Relevant industry, regulatory and other **external factors** including applicable reporting framework
- **Nature** of the entity
- Applicable **financial reporting framework** and **accounting policies**
- Entity's objectives and strategies and related **business risks** that could lead to material misstatement
- **Measurement** and review of the entity's **financial performance**
- How **inherent risk factors** affect the susceptibility of assertions to misstatement
- Entity's **system of internal control**

The entity's system of internal control

- **Control environment**, and whether this provides an appropriate foundation for the system of internal control
- Entity's **risk assessment process**, which should be appropriate to the entity's circumstances/nature/complexity
- Entity's **process to monitor** internal controls
- Entity's **information system and communication**, including the **IT environment**
- **Control activities**, including controls for **significant risks** (see 'Risk' tab) and controls for **risks arising from use of IT**

Control deficiencies

- Auditor to determine whether there are **any control deficiencies**

Analytical procedures: evaluation of financial information through analysis of plausible relationships among both financial and non-financial data.

Consider comparisons with

- Prior periods
- Anticipated results
- Similar industry information

Consider relationships between

- Financial and non-financial information
- Elements of financial information expected to follow pattern

ISA (UK) 315 Revised requires auditors to apply analytical procedures as part of risk assessment procedures at the planning stage.

Materiality

Guidance on materiality is given in ISA (UK) 320.

Materiality and audit risks are considered when:

- **Identifying and assessing the risks** of material misstatements;
- Determining the nature, timing and extent of **audit procedures**; and
- Evaluating the **effect of misstatements**

Assessing materiality helps auditors to judge:

- What/how many items to test
- Whether to use sampling techniques
- Level of error leading to modification of audit opinion

These should be reassessed during the audit due to changes in accounts/risk assessments.

Auditors also apply **performance materiality** in relation to specific transactions and balances. Performance materiality is **always lower than overall materiality.**

In order to calculate a level of materiality, the auditors will often take a range of values and use an average or weighted average, for example:

Profit before tax
5%
Revenue
0.5–1%
Total assets
1–2%

Audit risk = inherent risk $\times$ control risk $\times$ detection risk

Audit risk: the risk that the auditors give an inappropriate opinion on the FS.

Control risk: the risk that a misstatement that could occur in an assertion about a class of transactions, account balance or disclosure and that could be material, either individually or when aggregated with other misstatements, will not be prevented, or detected and corrected, on a timely basis by the entity's controls.

Inherent risk: the susceptibility of an assertion about a class of transaction, account balance or disclosure to a misstatement that could be material, either individually or when aggregated with other misstatements, before consideration of any related internal controls.

Detection risk: the risk that the procedures performed by the auditor to reduce audit risk to an acceptably low level will not detect a misstatement that exists and that could be material, either individually or when aggregated with other misstatements.

3: Process of assurance: planning the assignment

Significant risks

- Risk of fraud
- Related to recent significant economic, accounting or other development
- Complex transaction
- Significant transaction with related party
- High degree of subjectivity
- Unusual transaction

1 **Identify risks** throughout the process of obtaining an understanding of the entity.

2 **Relate the risks** to what can go wrong at the assertion level.

3 **Consider** whether the risks are of a **magnitude** that could result in a **material misstatement**.

4 **Consider** the **likelihood** of the risks causing a **material misstatement**.

Fraud

An intentional act by one or more individuals among management, those charged with governance, employees, or third parties, involving the use of deception to obtain an unjust or illegal advantage.

Characteristics of fraud

Fraud includes:

- Fraudulent financial reporting
- Misappropriation of assets

Error

An unintentional misstatement in financial statements, including the omission of an amount or a disclosure.

Responsibilities

Management and those charged with governance are responsible for prevention and detection. **Auditors** must be aware of the possibility of misstatement due to fraud.

ISA 315 UK (Revised) requires there to be a **discussion** of where fraud might take place.

Notes

4: Process of assurance: evidence and reporting

This chapter describes the basics of evidence collection. Evidence is necessary to justify the conclusion of the assurance report.

ISA (UK) 500, *Audit Evidence* gives guidance:

Sufficiency and appropriateness are **interrelated** and apply to both **tests of controls** and **substantive** procedures.

ISA (UK) 500.4

The objective of the auditor is to design and perform audit procedures in such a way as to enable the auditor to obtain sufficient appropriate audit evidence to be able to draw reasonable conclusions on which to base the auditor's opinion.

Sufficiency
Quantity

Appropriateness
Quality

You may be asked how strong specific evidence is

Influenced by:

- Risk assessment
- Nature of systems
- Materiality of item
- Experience
- Source and reliability
- Results of procedures

External evidence (more reliable than internal)

Auditor evidence (obtained directly by auditors better than that obtained from entity)

Entity evidence (more reliable when controls effective)

Written evidence (more reliable than oral)

Original evidence (more reliable than photocopies)

Assertions	Audit procedures

Assertions

- About classes of transactions and events, and related disclosures

  (Occurrence, completeness, accuracy, cut-off, classification, presentation)

- About account balances, and related disclosures, at the period-end

  (Existence, rights and obligations, completeness, accuracy, valuation and allocation, classification, presentation)

Audit procedures

- **Inspection** of assets
- **Inspection** of documentation
- **Observation**
- **Inquiry**
- **Confirmation**
- **Recalculation/reperformance**
- **Analytical procedures**

Test of controls	The auditor needs evidence about the **operating effectiveness** of controls.
Substantive procedures	Audit procedures performed to detect material misstatements at the assertion level. The auditor **must always** carry out substantive procedures on **material items**.

4: Process of assurance: evidence and reporting

Auditor's reports in the UK are governed by ISA (UK) 700, *Forming an Opinion and Reporting on Financial Statements* and the FRC's Bulletin (2020).

Contents of the auditor's report in the UK

- Title
- Addressee
- **Auditor's opinion** section comes first, with the heading 'Opinion', expressing an opinion on the financial statements
- **Basis for opinion** section
- **Going concern** section
- **Key audit matters** section, for audits of listed companies
- **Other information** section
- **Responsibilities of management for the financial statements** section
- **Auditor's responsibilities for the audit of the financial statements** section
- **Opinion on other matters**
- Matters on which the auditor is required to **report by exception**
- **Name** of engagement partner
- **Signature** of engagement partner
- Auditor's **address**
- **Date** of the report

5: Introduction to internal control

Internal controls are discussed in ISA (UK) 315 Revised, Identifying and Assessing the Risks of Material Misstatements.

Internal controls are a key topic area and this chapter is essential background.

Components of internal control	Computer controls	Limitations of internal control	Recording internal controls

System of internal control: the process designed, implemented and maintained by those charged with governance, management and other personnel, to provide reasonable assurance about the achievement of an entity's objectives with regard to reliability of financial reporting, effectiveness and efficiency of operations, and compliance with applicable laws and regulations.

Internal controls may prevent an error occurring (preventative control), or may identify that an error has occurred and correct it (detective control).

Components of internal control

- Control environment
- Risk assessment process
- Monitoring process
- Information system and communication
- Control activities

Relevant controls

Not all controls are relevant to the auditor's risk assessment. The auditor is primarily concerned with those which are part of the management of risk that may give rise to a material misstatement in the FS.

Control environment: includes the attitudes, awareness and actions of management and those charged with governance concerning the entity's internal control and its importance in the entity. The control environment also includes the governance and management functions and sets the tone of an organisation, influencing the control consciousness of its people. It is the foundation for effective internal control, providing discipline and structure.

An audit committee is an important aspect of the control environment of the company.

It is comprised of non-executive directors and is a requirement in UK listed companies.

Audit committees

- Review integrity of company FS and formal announcements relating to company performance
- Monitor and review effectiveness of company's internal audit function
- Make recommendations to board in relation to the external auditor
- Monitor independence of external auditor
- Implement policy on provision of non-audit services by external auditor
- Review company's internal financial controls and risk management systems (unless a separate risk management committee exists)

Components of internal control	Computer controls	Limitations of internal control	Recording internal controls

Business risk: a risk resulting from significant conditions, events, circumstances, actions or inactions that could adversely affect an entity's ability to achieve its objectives and execute its strategies, or from the setting of inappropriate objectives and strategies.

Entity's risk assessment process

Identify relevant business risks → Estimate the impact of risks → Assess the likelihood of occurrence

Decide upon actions (internal controls, insurances, changes in operations) to address them

Control activity	Explanation/example
Authorisation and approval	Approval of transactions/documents
Reconciliations	Comparison of two or more data elements
Verifications	Comparison of two or more items with each other or with a policy
Physical or logical controls	Physical security of assets, and access to computer systems/data files
Segregation of duties	Assigning different individuals the responsibilities of authorising transactions, recording transactions and maintaining custody of assets

In an IT environment, there are two important types of control.

General IT controls: Controls over the entity's IT processes that support the continued proper operation of the IT environment, including the continued effective functioning of information processing controls and the integrity of information (ie, the completeness, accuracy and validity of information) in the entity's information system.

Information processing controls: Controls relating to the processing of information in IT applications or manual information processes in the entity's information system that directly address risks to the integrity of information (ie, the completeness, accuracy and validity of transactions and other information).

General IT controls should be audited before information processing controls since information processing controls will be of little use if the general IT controls are ineffective.

Cyber security risks are an ever increasing risk for most organisations and include:

- Human threats
- Fraud
- Deliberate sabotage
- Viruses and other corruptions
- Malware
- Denial of service (DoS) attacks

The ICAEW suggests that an organisation appoint a **chief information security officer** to assume ultimate responsibility for managing cyber risks however this may be difficult for small and medium sized enterprises.

Internal control provides directors with only reasonable assurance that objectives are met, because internal control has inherent limitations.

- Costs of control outweigh the benefit
- Potential for **human error**
- Possibility of collusion in fraud between employees
- Controls could be bypassed/ overridden by management
- Controls are designed to cope with routine transactions not non-routine ones

Small companies

Small companies find it harder to implement effective systems of internal control as they generally have fewer employees than larger companies. This makes segregation of duties more difficult.

Hence segregation of duties is vital

5: Introduction to internal control

Components of internal control	Computer controls	Limitations of internal control	Recording internal controls

Notes

Good for:
- Simple systems
- Background information

Disadvantages:
- Not good for complex systems

Checklists

Good for:
- Making sure cover everything

Disadvantages:
- Relevant questions may not be on checklist
- Discourage thinking

Diagrams

Good for:
- Recording relationships and reporting lines

Disadvantages:
- Time consuming to construct
- Can be difficult for reader to assimilate

6: Revenue system

It is important to be comfortable with:

- Examples of controls for specific transaction areas
- What the control is trying to achieve (objective)

Some examples of tests of controls have been given in this chapter. However, they are not exhaustive. Remember that the test is seeking to establish whether the control is effective. If you bear that in mind you should be able to tailor tests of controls to the specific scenario in the question.

Sales system

Aims of control

Ordering

- Sales made to customers with good credit ratings
- Customers are encouraged to pay promptly
- Orders are correct
- Orders are fulfilled

Despatch/invoicing

- All despatches are recorded
- Invoicing is correct and for goods supplied
- Credit notes given are for valid reasons

Recording

- Transactions are recorded
  - In correct accounts
  - In correct period
- Irrecoverable receivables identified

Controls

Ordering

- Segregation of duties (credit control/invoice/despatch)
- Authorisation of credit terms (checks obtained and reviewed)
- Sequential numbering of pre-printed order forms
- Correct prices quoted to customers
- Match orders to despatch records (o/s orders queried)
- Dealing with customer queries

Despatch/invoicing

- Authorisation of despatch
- Examination of goods despatched (quality)
- Recording of goods outward
- Match despatch records to order/invoice (o/s queried)
- Sequential numbering of pre-printed despatch records
- Signature of customer on despatch records
- Authorisation of price on invoice (price list)
- Arithmetical checks on invoices

Recording

- Segregation of duties (recording sales/statements)
- Recording of sequence of sales invoices
- Matching cash receipts with invoices
- Retention of customer remittance advices
- Preparation/checking of receivables statements
- Review/chase overdue accounts/authorised write-off

Tests of control

Ordering

Check for evidence of:

- References
- Authorisation
- Credit terms/limits not breached
- Orders matched to despatch records and production orders

Despatch/Invoicing

- Agree despatch records to sales invoice
- Agree sales to inventory records
- Verify non-routine sales
- Verify credit notes
- Test numerical sequence of despatch records, invoices, credit notes and order forms and enquire into missing numbers
- Check any special terms authorised by management

Recording

- Check entries in nominal ledger to invoices, check additions and postings to nominal ledger
- Check credit limits observed
- Check overdue accounts chased
- Check irrecoverable debts written off are authorised
- Check trade receivable statements regularly sent
- Check control accounts reconciled regularly

Cash system

Aims of control

- All monies received are banked, recorded and safeguarded against loss/theft.
- All payments are authorised, made out to the correct payees and recorded.
- Payments are not made twice for the same liability.

Controls

Receipts

- Segregation of duties
- Safeguards at post opening (two people/listing)
- Post stamped with date of receipt
- Restrictions on receipt of cash (sales people only)
- Agreement of cash collections to till rolls
- Prompt maintenance of records
- Giving and recording receipts for cash

Bank

- Daily bankings, banking of receipts intact
- Restrictions on opening new bank accounts
- Limitations on cash floats
- Surprise cash counts
- Custody of cash and cheques
- Restrictions on issuing blank cheques
- Bank reconciliations

Payments

- Cheque requisitions supported by documentation/authorised
- Authorised signatories
- Prompt dispatch of signed cheques
- Payments recorded promptly
- Cash payments authorised
- Limit on disbursements
- Rules on cash advances to employees

Test of control

- Observe post opening. Trace entries on listing to cash account, paying-in book, bank statement
- Verify till receipts to cash sale summaries, check to paying-in slip
- Check cash is banked daily
- Check cash receipts from cash account to paying-in slips, bank, posting to the nominal ledger
- For cash payments, check that electronic transfers are authorised by approved individuals, and that any cheques are signed by authorised signatories (paid cheques can be requested from the bank). Check to supplier invoice, verify that supporting documents are stamped 'paid'
- Check postings to the nominal ledger
- Reperform a bank reconciliation
- Observe a cash count

Notes

7: Purchases system

The purchases system is an important system in a business. Your assessment could include scenario internal controls questions in this area.

Purchases system

Aims of control

Ordering
- Orders are authorised and for the company
- Made from authorised suppliers
- At good prices

Receipt/Invoice
- Only accepted if from authorised order
- Accurately recorded
- Liabilities recognised for goods received
- Credits are claimed

Payment
- Expenditure is only for received goods
- Authorised
- Properly recorded
- In correct account
- In correct period

Controls		
Ordering	**Receipt/invoice**	**Payment**
■ Segregation of duties (requisitioning/ordering)	■ Examine goods inwards (quality) and record deliveries	■ Segregation of duties (recording/checking)
■ Central policy for choice of supplier	■ Compare goods received records (GRR) with orders	■ Prompt recording in nominal ledger
■ Use of pre-numbered purchase requisitions	■ Reference suppliers' invoices	■ Comparison of supplier statements to supplier balance in trade payables account
■ Authorised, pre-numbered (safeguarded) order forms	■ Check suppliers' invoices (maths, prices, quantities)	■ Authorisation of payments (limits/goods received)
■ Monitoring of supplier terms for most favourable	■ Record goods returns	■ Review of allocation of expenditure
	■ Have procedures for obtaining credit notes	■ Procedures for cut-off

Tests of control

- It is vital that auditors check that all invoices are supported by genuine purchase orders, authorised by correct individual. Check invoices are supported by GRRs, priced correctly, coded correctly, entered in inventory, maths correct, posted to nominal ledger

- Check numerical sequences

- Check entries to nominal ledger

- Check that the payables account contains no unusual entries

8: Employee costs

The payroll system is another important practical area.

Some examples of tests of controls have been given in this chapter. However, they are not exhaustive.

Remember the best approach is seeking to establish whether the control is effective.

TP06-1122-061

Wages
system

Aims of control

Calculating

- Only paid for work done
- Gross and net pay calculated correctly
- Gross pay authorised

Recording

- Gross pay, net pay and deductions accurately recorded
- Wages paid recorded correctly in bank and cash records and nominal ledger
- All deductions authorised and calculated correctly
- Correct amounts paid to HMRC

Payment

- Correct employees paid

Controls		

Calculating
- Segregation of duties
- Regular checking of wages to personnel records
- Authorisation
- Timesheets/clocking in and out
- Recording of changes
- Review of hours worked
- Review of wages against budget

Recording
- Segregation of duties
- Automatic checks
- Basis for compilation of payroll
- Check payroll details to personnel records
- Reconcile total pay and deductions from one period to the next
- Agree tax deducted to tax returns
- Procedures for non-routine matters

Cash payment
- Segregation of duties
- Authorisation wage cheques
- Custody of cash
- Verification of identity
- Recording of distribution

Non-cash payment
- Authorisation of bank transfer lists
- Comparison of bank transfer list to payroll
- Maintenance and reconciliation of wages and salaries control account

Tests of controls

Calculating

- Check wages summary approved
- Obtain evidence staff only start being paid when join company
- Obtain evidence staff are removed from payroll on leaving company
- Check pay calculations are checked
- Agree gross pay to clockcards/ time sheets and that overtime is authorised
- Agree salaries to personnel records

Recording

- Check total salaries have been reconciled to previous week/ month of the standard payroll
- Check payroll casts and has been posted correctly to nominal ledger
- Check payments to HMRC correct

Payment

- Attend a pay-out of cash wages and ensure procedures followed
- Check no employee receives more than one wage packet
- Check unclaimed wages are recorded, banked and explained
- Agree a certified copy of bank list to payroll net pay summary

9: Internal audit

Internal audit is an important control function in an organisation and an example of good corporate governance. This chapter looks at the best practice recommendations of the UK Corporate Governance Code in relation to the internal audit function, as well as contrasting the roles of internal and external audit.

Internal audit: an appraisal activity established or provided as a service to the entity. Its functions include, amongst other things, examining, evaluating and monitoring the adequacy and effectiveness of internal control.

International codes on corporate governance

The UK *Corporate Governance Code*, as an example of an internationally recognised code on corporate governance, recommends that the audit committee of a company should:

(a) Monitor and review effectiveness of internal audit activities

(b) If there is no internal audit function, consider annually whether there is need for one

(c) If there is no internal audit function, explain this absence in the annual report

Distinction between internal and external audit

	Purpose	Scope	Relationship to company	Reporting	Fraud
Internal	An activity designed to add value and improve an organisation's operations.	Internal audit's work relates to the operations of the organisation.	Internal auditors are often employees of the organisation, although sometimes the internal audit function is outsourced.	Internal auditors reports to senior management and audit committee.	Prevention and detection of fraud is management's responsibility. But internal auditors should be alert to risks and exposures that could allow fraud as they are involved in risk management.
External	An exercise to enable auditors to express an opinion on the financial statements.	External audit's work relates to the financial statements. They are concerned with the financial records that underlie these.	External auditors are independent of the company and its management. They are appointed by the shareholders.	Audit report addressed to the shareholders.	Prevention and detection of fraud is management's responsibility.

Activities

- Monitor internal controls
- Examine financial and operating information
- Review the economy, efficiency and effectiveness of operations
- Review compliance with laws, regulations and other external requirements
- Special investigations
- Identify and evaluating significant exposures to risk
- Assess the governance process

10: Documentation

Auditors must keep evidence of the work they have done, in the form of working papers. This chapter shows what these papers must contain, where they should be stored and who has a right of access to them.

Why use working papers?

- Evidence auditor has followed ISAs (UK)
- Supports opinion given on FS
- To facilitate quality control reviews
- Assist with planning
- Assist direction and supervision

Automated working papers can make the documenting of audit work much easier and can save time.

Contents of each paper

- Client name
- Reporting date
- Name and date of preparer
- Name and date of reviewer
- File reference and appropriate cross-referencing
- Subject
- Conclusions drawn and key points highlighted
- Objective of work done
- Source of information
- Information on sample size and selection
- Work done and results obtained
- Key to any symbols/audit ticks
- Analysis of errors

Permanent files

- Engagement letter
- New client questionnaire
- Memorandum
- Articles of association
- Legal documents
- History of business
- Board minutes of continuing relevance
- Prior period signed accounts, analytical procedures and management letters
- Accounting system notes
- Prior period control questionnaire

Current files

- Financial statements
- Account checklists
- Management accounts
- Reconciliation of management accounts to financial statements
- Summary of unadjusted errors
- Partner report
- Review notes
- Audit planning memorandum
- Time budgets and summaries
- Written representations from management
- Notes of board minutes
- Third party communications
- Working papers

Ownership

Working papers are the property of the assurance providers. The report becomes the property of the client once it has been issued.

Rights of access

Assurance providers are not required to show working papers to the client. However, they may be shown at their discretion.

Working papers should only be shown to third parties with the client's permission.

Files must be kept securely to ensure confidentially requirements are met.

| Paper documents | → | Locked premises |
| Electronic documents | → | Electronic controls |

The ICAEW requires audit working papers to be kept for at least six years from the end of the accounting period to which they relate.

11: Evidence and sampling

Topic List

Accounting estimates

Sampling

CAATs

In this chapter we look at the audit of accounting estimates, and the use of sampling and CAATs when carrying out audit procedures.

CAATs	Sampling	**Accounting estimates**

Accounting estimate: A monetary amount for which the measurement, in accordance with the requirements of the applicable financial reporting framework, is subject to estimation uncertainty.

Estimation uncertainty is the 'susceptibility to an inherent lack of precision in measurement'.

(ISA (UK) 540: para. 12)

Guidance is given in ISA (UK) 540, *Audit of Accounting Estimates and Related Disclosures.*

Nature

These estimates may be simple and relatively low-risk, but they may also be highly complex and require management to make significant judgments to apply IFRS, eg, in the case of complex financial instruments.

Audit procedures

Procedures should be responsive to both control risk, and to the degree of inherent risk. They include:

- Testing management processes and data
- Using an auditor's point estimate or range
- Reviewing events occurring up to the date of the auditor's report
- Testing the operating effectiveness of controls over the production of estimates, together with substantive procedures
- Reperforming the estimate, eg, where controls are not likely to be effective

Evaluation

The auditor should 'stand back', and make a final decision on reasonableness based on other audit evidence.

Sampling is a **key aspect of obtaining sufficient appropriate audit evidence**. A sample must be chosen which enables the auditor to get the evidence he needs. Guidance is given in ISA (UK) 530, *Audit Sampling*.

The ISA looks at four aspects of sampling:

- Design of the sample
- Size of the sample
- Selecting the sample
- Draw conclusions from the sample

→ Auditors are faced with sampling risk in both tests of controls and substantive procedures.

Sampling: applying audit procedures to <100% of items in a population.

Tolerable misstatement: a monetary amount set by the auditor; actual misstatements should not exceed this.

Sampling risk: the risk that the auditor's conclusion based on a sample is different from what it would have been if 100% tested.

Non-sampling risk: the risk that inappropriate audit procedures are chosen regardless of sample, or that results are misunderstood.

Design

The auditor should consider:

- The purpose of the audit procedure
- The characteristics of the population
- The sampling method
- The selection method

Size

Consider **sampling risk** and **tolerable misstatement**.

The auditor must use professional **judgement** to assess **audit risk** and design audit **procedures** to ensure that this **risk** is **reduced** to an **acceptably low level**. In determining sample size, the auditor should consider whether sampling risk is reduced to an acceptably low level. ISA (UK) 530 gives some relevant factors in an appendix.

Two testing procedures do not involve sampling:

- Testing 100% of items in a population

- Testing all items with certain characteristics

Methods

(a) **Random**: all items have equal chance of selection

(b) **Systematic**: constant interval between items

(c) **Haphazard**: chosen at will, but guarding against bias in the selection

(d) **MUS (monetary unit sampling)**: sampling unit is the individual monetary unit in the population

(e) **Sequence/block selection**: consecutive items

Auditors must analyse any misstatements in the sample and draw inferences for the population as a whole.

Qualitative aspects of the misstatement are also considered, including the **nature** and **cause** of the misstatement.

Statistical sampling: involves **random** selection and **probability** theory to evaluate results.

Non-statistical sampling: does not use statistical methods and uses **judgement** to evaluate results.

It is now the norm for both businesses and auditors to make significant use of **computers**. IT brings many advantages to audit, particularly in areas such as analytical review.

CAATs: audit techniques performed using computers, which can enhance the detail of the test undertaken and the result of the test. They consist of **audit software** and **test data**.

Audit software

This performs checks that auditors would otherwise have had to do by hand.

- Extracting a sample according to specified criteria
- Calculate ratios and select those outside set criteria
- Check calculations
- Prepare reports
- Follow items through a system and flag where they are posted

Test data

This is a way of **checking whether client systems are operating properly:** feed the system some data to see how it is processed.

The data may be valid or invalid, depending on the objective of the test.

Data analytics

When used to obtain audit evidence in a financial statement audit, data analytics is the science and art of discovering and analysing patterns, deviations and inconsistencies, and extracting other useful information in the data underlying or related to the subject matter of an audit through analysis, modelling and visualisation for the purpose of planning and performing the audit.

Data analytics are a development from CAATs. Part of the 'big data' revolution, they allow auditors to use **standardised software** to analyse a client's transactions, and to present this analysis in intuitive new ways.

Examples of areas where this may be used include:

- To analyse all transactions in a population, stratify that population and identify outliers for further examination
- To reperform calculations relevant to the financial statements
- To match transactions as they pass through a processing cycle
- To assist in segregation of duties testing
- To compare entity data to externally obtained data
- To manipulate data to assess the impact of different assumptions.   (FRC, 2017: p7)

Notes

12: Written representations

Written representations are only a useful source of evidence for certain transactions where little evidence exists, and should be treated with caution.

Auditors receive many representations during the course of an audit, and **some may be critical** to obtaining sufficient, appropriate audit evidence. An example, which the auditors must get, is acknowledgement from the directors of their responsibility for the financial statements which the auditors have audited.

Guidance is given in ISA 580, *Written Representations.*

Types of written representation

- Management responsibilities
- Specific written representations required by other ISAs (UK)
- Where necessary to support other audit evidence

Representations by management as audit evidence

ISA 580.4 Although written representations provide necessary audit evidence, they do not provide sufficient appropriate audit evidence on their own about any of the matters with which they deal.

Written representations cannot be used instead of other (better) evidence which the auditors expect to exist.

Basic elements of a written representation letter

The letter should be: addressed to the auditors, contain specified information, appropriately dated, approved by those who have the specific knowledge. Auditors will normally request that the letter is signed by a senior executive officer/senior financial officer.

The auditor will need to consider:

- The reliability of written representations
- Whether written representations are consistent with other audit evidence

Notes

13: Substantive procedures – key financial statement figures

Topic List

Non-current assets

Inventory

Receivables

Bank

Payables

Long-term liabilities

In practice, inventory is a very important audit area. For manufacturing businesses it is often the largest item on the statement of financial position, and is usually material. Other areas such as receivables and payables will be an important audit area for every business.

These areas can be difficult to audit. These balances often comprise of lots of small items, which can make them time-consuming to audit.

| Non-current assets | Inventory | Receivables | Bank | Payables | Long-term liabilities |

Tangible non-current assets: physical assets held for continuing use in the business. Examples of tangible non-current assets include land, buildings, plant, vehicles, fittings and equipment.

Intangible non-current assets: examples include licenses, development costs and purchased brands.

Internal control considerations

- Acquisitions are authorised and recorded
- Disposals are authorised and recorded
- Proceeds are accounted for
- Security over non-current assets sufficient
- Non-current assets maintained properly
- Depreciation reviewed annually
- Is a register kept?
- Does the company actually own the assets?
- Do the assets exist?
- Assets over/undervalued?
- Are assets correctly presented in the financial statements?

Completeness

Obtain a schedule from the client, reconcile it to last year's schedules. **Reconcile** the list of assets in the **nominal ledger** with those in the **non-current asset register**. Obtain explanations for missing assets. Test some physical assets to ensure they are recorded.

Existence

Confirm that the company physically inspects all the assets in the register annually. **Inspect assets**. (Do they exist? What's their condition? Are they in use?) Reconcile opening and closing motor vehicles by numbers as well as by value.

Valuation

Verify valuation to purchase invoice or **valuation certificate** (consider reasonableness of valuation). Check any **revaluation surplus** has been **correctly calculated**. Check that revaluations are updated regularly.

Rights and obligations

Verify title to **land** by checking **title deeds/leases**. Obtain certificate from people holding deeds to confirm why they are held. Inspect **registration documents for vehicles**, confirm that they are **used for the business**. Examine documents of title for other assets.

Presentation and disclosure

Review financial statements to ensure disclosure requirements have been met.

Charges and commitments (rights)

Review statutory books for evidence of charges, examine post year-end invoices and board minutes for evidence of any capital commitments.

Disposals (rights, existence)

Verify disposals to **sales documentation** (invoice) and check **calculation of profit/loss** is correct. Check that disposals are **authorised** and proceeds are reasonable. Ensure that asset is no longer used as security.

Non-current assets	Inventory	Receivables	Bank	Payables	Long-term liabilities

Additions (rights/valuation/completeness)

Check additions to invoices/architect's certificates etc. Check purchases properly allocated to asset accounts and authorised by correct person and that all additions have been recorded in the nominal ledger and the asset register.

Depreciation (valuation)

Review depreciation rates in light of: asset lives, residual values, replacement policy, past experience (consistency), possible obsolescence. **Check** that **depreciation has been charged** on all assets with a useful economic life. **Check calculation**. Ensure depreciation not charged on fully depreciated assets. Check that rates and policies are disclosed in the FS. Check that depreciation on revalued assets is based on the revalued amount.

Insurance (valuation)

Review insurance policies in force for all assets to ensure cover is sufficient and check expiry dates.

Planning inventory count

- **Gain knowledge** (previous year) and discuss major changes with management.
- **Assess key factors** (such as nature of inventories, high value items, accounting, location, controls).
- **Plan procedures** (time/location of attendance, high value items, any specialist help, third party confirmations required?)

Review inventory count instructions

Ensure there is provision for:

- **Organisation of count** (supervision, marking of inventories, control during the process, identification of obsolete inventories).
- **Counting** (systematic counting to ensure all inventories are counted, usually by teams of two counters one independent of inventories usually).
- **Recording** (control over inventory sheets, ink used, signed by counters).

During inventory count

- Check **instructions** are followed.
- Make **test counts** for accuracy.
- Check procedures for **obsolete** inventories.
- Confirm **third party** inventories separate.
- Conclude whether inventory count has been **properly carried out.**
- Gain overall **impression** of inventories.

After inventory count

- Trace **test count** items to final inventory sheets.
- **All** count records **included** in final total?
- Confirm **cut-off** using final goods in and out records.
- Check replies from **third parties.**
- Confirm **valuation.**

| Non-current assets | Inventory | Receivables | Bank | Payables | Long-term liabilities |

Remember: inventories should be valued at the lower of cost and net realisable value (IAS 2).

Original cost (All types of inventories)

The auditors must ensure that the **method** is **allowed** under law and standards, **consistent, calculated correctly**.

Actual costs can be checked by referring to **supplier invoices**.

The auditor should bear in mind the **age** of inventories when considering cost.

Production cost (WIP and FG)

Cost is the cost of purchase + **cost of conversion**.

The auditors may be able to use **analytical procedures** to assess the costs of conversion.

Material: check to invoices and price lists.

Labour: check to wage records/time summaries.

Overheads: allocation consistent and based on normal production.

NRV (All types of inventories)

Auditors should compare cost/ NRV. **NRV is likely to be lower** than **cost** where:

- Costs increasing
- Inventories deteriorated
- Inventories obsolete
- Marketing strategy dictates
- Errors made

The auditors should follow up **obsolete items** and **review prices** and strategies.

Receivables listing/age analysis

Much of the detailed work will be carried out on a sample of **receivables balances**. Ideally, this will be **aged**, showing amounts owed and from when they are owed.

External confirmation

Verification of trade receivables by direct confirmation from customers is the normal method of getting audit evidence to check the **existence** and **rights and obligations** of trade receivables.

Positive method: customer is requested to confirm the accuracy of the balance shown or state in what respect he is in disagreement (preferable method).

Negative method: customer is requested only to reply if the amount stated is disputed.

The circularisation letter is generally **prepared by the client**, but the customer should **reply to the auditor**.

Sample selection	Follow up, where:

Sample selection

Special attention to:

- Old unpaid accounts
- Accounts written-off in period
- Accounts with credit balances
- Accounts settled by round sum payments

Do not overlook:

- Nil balances
- Accounts paid by the time of the audit

Follow up, where:

- Customers disagree with the balance
- Customers do not respond (positive method only)

Reasons for disagreements: disputes, cut-off problems, receipt sent before year-end but received afterwards, mis-posting, customers netting off credits and debits, teeming and lading frauds. The auditor should investigate the reasons for disagreement.

Alternative procedures (where no response arrives):

Second (and third) requests should be sent to the customer in the first instance. Then the auditors should involve credit controller to chase the debt, and do other tests.

Auditor may check the receipt of cash after date, verify purchase orders, and test the company's control over irrecoverable debts

The audit of bank will need to cover **completeness, existence, rights and obligations,** and allocation and **valuation.**

All these elements can be audited through the **bank letter** (example below). This is a standard document.

Banks will require:

- Explicit written authority from client
- Auditors' request must refer to it
- Request must reach the bank two weeks before the year-end

Procedures

- Obtain bank confirmations
- Check the arithmetic of the bank reconciliation
- Trace payments or cheques shown as outstanding to the after date bank statements
- Trace receipts shown as outstanding to after date bank statements
- Review previous bank reconciliation to ensure all amounts are cleared
- Obtain explanations for items in bank statements, not cash account and *vice versa*
- Verify balances on reconciliation to bank letter and cash account
- Scrutinise the cash account for unusual items, or consider performing data analytics routines where appropriate

Auditors should be aware of the possibility of understatement of payables.

There are **two detailed objectives** with regard to trade payables:

- Is cut-off correct between goods received and invoices received?
- Do trade payables represent the *bona fide* amounts due by the company?

Completeness, rights and obligations, existence

The key test is a comparison of supplier statements with the nominal ledger balances. Supplier statements are third party evidence.

However, it is sometimes necessary to **circularise suppliers**. Examples of such situations are:

- Supplier statements are unavailable/incomplete
- Internal controls are weak and material misstatement of liabilities is feared as a consequence
- Suspicion that client is understating deliberately

Long-term liabilities: those due after more than one year. Usually they are debentures, loan stock and bank loans.

The key financial statement assertions are:

(a) **Completeness**: whether all long-term liabilities have been disclosed

(b) **Accuracy and cut-off**: whether interest payable has been calculated correctly and included in the right period

(c) **Disclosure**: whether long-term loans are correctly disclosed

Audit procedures

- Obtain/prepare a schedule of loans
- Agree opening balances to prior year and check the clerical accuracy
- Compare the balances to the nominal ledger
- Check lenders to any register of lenders (eg, debenture holders)
- Trace additions and repayments to cash account
- Confirm repayment conforms to agreement
- Verify borrowing limits per the articles are not exceeded
- Obtain direct confirmation from lenders
- Review minutes and cash account to ensure that all loans have been included

14: Codes of professional ethics

Topic List

ICAEW Code

FRC *Ethical Standard*

When approaching questions on ethics, follow a three-stage strategy:

- *What do the fundamental principles say?*
- *What does the detailed guidance say?*
- *What does my common sense/practical experience tell me?*

Code of Ethics and Conduct

Guidance is in the form of **fundamental principles** (see below), specific guidance and explanatory notes.

Integrity	To be **straightforward** and **honest** in all business and professional relationships.
Objectivity	To **not compromise professional or business judgments** because of bias, conflicts of interest or undue influence of others.
Professional competence and due care	To attain and maintain **professional knowledge** and **skill** at the level required to ensure that a client or employing organisation receives **competent professional service**, based on current technical and professional standards and relevant legislation; and to **act diligently** and in accordance with **applicable** technical and professional standards.
Confidentiality	To **respect** the **confidentiality** of information acquired as a result of professional and business relationships.
Professional behaviour	To **comply** with relevant **laws and regulations** and to avoid any action that the professional accountant knows or should know might discredit the profession.

Threats to independence	Safeguards

Threats to independence

- Self interest
- Self review
- Advocacy
- Familiarity
- Intimidation
- Management

ICAEW code incorporates the IESBA *Code of Ethics* and contains additional rules deemed appropriate by the ICAEW.

Safeguards

Created by profession, legislation or regulation:

- Entry requirements into profession
- CPD
- Corporate governance regulations
- Professional standards
- Professional/regulatory monitoring and disciplinary procedures
- External review

In work environment:

- Review of work done
- Consulting an independent third party
- Rotating senior personnel
- Discussing ethical issues with those charged with governance

FRC Ethical Standard

The FRC *Ethical Standard* contains guidance in the following areas.

- Section 1: General Requirements and Guidance
- Section 2: Financial, Business, Employment and Personal Relationships
- Section 3: Long Association with Engagements and with Entities Relevant to Engagements
- Section 4: Fees, Remuneration and Evaluation Policies, Gifts and Hospitality, Litigation
- Section 5: Non-audit/Additional Services

15: Integrity, objectivity and independence

Integrity, objectivity and independence are fundamental qualities the auditor must possess. This chapter looks at potential threats to these principles and ways to reduce them.

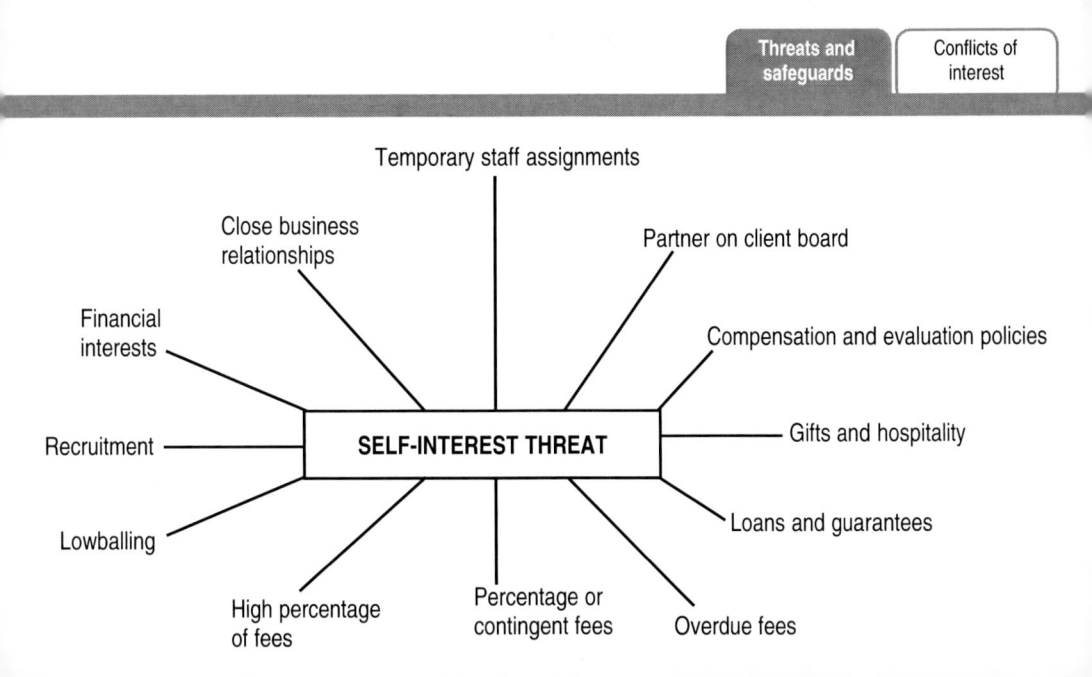

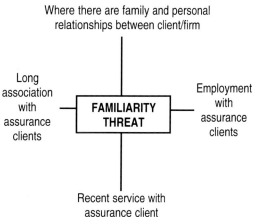

Advocacy threat

- Legal services
- Contingent fees
- Corporate finance

Intimidation threat

- Close business relationships
- Actual and threatened litigation
- Assurance staff members moving to employment with client
- Family and personal relationships

A management threat arises when the audit firm undertakes work involving making judgements and taking decisions that are the responsibility of management.

The FRC *Ethical Standard* features stricter rules for auditors of public interest entities (PIEs) than for non-PIEs. Auditors of PIEs are **prohibited** from providing the following services:

- **Tax services** in certain areas (eg, preparation of tax forms, payroll, tax advice)
- Services that involve playing any part in the management
- **Bookkeeping** and preparing **accounting records** and **financial statements**
- **Payroll** services
- Designing and implementing **internal control** or **risk management** procedures related to the preparation of financial information
- **Valuation** services
- **Legal** services
- **Internal audit** services
- Corporate finance services
- Promoting, dealing in, or underwriting **shares** in the audited entity
- **Human resources** services

(FRC *Ethical Standard*: Appendix B)

Accountants in industry are more likely to face a conflict of interest than accountants in practice.

1   Resolve internally (if possible) using formal dispute resolution process or audit committee

2   Obtain advice from ICAEW

3   Obtain advice from legal counsel

4   Resign (as a last resort)

It is always preferable to resolve conflicts 'in-house' where possible.

16: Confidentiality

Confidentiality is a fundamental principle. This chapter gives guidance on safeguards and situations where disclosure is allowed.

Safeguards

- Do not discuss client matters with any party outside accountancy firm
- Do not discuss client matters with colleagues in a public place
- Do not leave audit files unattended
- Do not leave audit files in cars or unsecured private residences
- Do not remove working papers from office unless strictly necessary
- Do not work on client files on unprotected computers

The professional duty of confidentiality

Exam focus

Information gained from professional work should not be disclosed unless:

- Consent obtained from client;
- There is a public duty to disclose; or
- A legal/professional right/duty to disclose.

  └── A member should not use (or appear to use) information for his own or some other's benefit.

Exceptions to the prohibition on disclosure:

Disclosure
■ Where disclosure is **permitted** by law and the client agrees, eg, reporting fraud to the police
■ Where disclosure is **required** by law, eg, client is involved in terrorist activities, breaches of FCA regulation, or suspicions of money laundering
■ Where there is a **professional duty** or right to disclose, when not prohibited by law, eg, in a negligence claim

Safeguards | Disclosure

Money laundering

- Criminal offence not to report suspicion
- Suspect must not be made aware of any investigation (need to avoid 'tipping off')
- Audit firms must have a nominated officer and a Money Laundering Reporting Officer (MLRO), who can be the same individual person
- Audit staff must report any suspicion to MLRO
- This does not constitute a breach of confidentiality

Conflicts of interest

- Consideration in accepting new assignments
- Threat to objectivity/confidentiality
- May be managed with appropriate safeguards
- Test of reasonable and informed observer
- Where conflict is not manageable, refuse assignment/cease to act

Notes

Notes